MOON

Brightest Object in the Night Sky

by J. Clark Sawyer

Consultant: Karly M. Pitman, PhD
Planetary Science Institute
Tucson, Arizona

BEARPORT
PUBLISHING

New York, New York

Credits

Cover, © NASA/JPL/USGS; TOC, © Gregory H. Revera/Wikipedia; 4–5, © NASA/JPL/ USGS; 6–7, © Wikipedia & NASA; 8, © Gregory H. Revera/Wikipedia; 9, © NASA; 10–11, © Wikipedia & NASA; 12, © Peter Freiman/Wikipedia; 13, © NASA/SDO (AIA); 14, © Jorge Salcedo/Shutterstock; 15, © Sinelyov/Shutterstock; 16–17, © NASA; 18, © NASA; 19, © NASA; 20, © NASA; 21, © Shannon Moore/Wikipedia; 23TL, © NASA; 23TM, © NASA Earth Observatory; 23TR, © NASA; 23BL, © Groomee/iStockphoto; 23BM, © Groomee Photography/iStockphoto; 23BR, © NASA/Wikipedia.

Publisher: Kenn Goin
Editor: Jessica Rudolph
Creative Director: Spencer Brinker
Design: Deborah Kaiser
Photo Researcher: Michael Win

Library of Congress Cataloging-in-Publication Data

Clark Sawyer, J., author.
  Our moon : brightest object in the night sky / by J. Clark Sawyer.
      pages cm. — (Out of this world)
  Includes bibliographical references and index.
  ISBN 978-1-62724-570-8 (library binding) — ISBN 1-62724-570-7 (library binding)
  1. Moon—Juvenile literature. I. Title.
  QB582.C56 2015
  523.3—dc23
                                      2014034611

For more information, write to Bearport Publishing Company, Inc., 45 West 21st Street, Suite 3B, New York, New York 10010. Printed in the United States of America.

10 9 8 7 6 5 4 3 2 1

CONTENTS

What is the brightest
object in the night sky?

OUR MOON!

The Moon is part of Earth's Solar System.

MARS

VENUS

MERCURY

JUPITER

SUN

MOON

EARTH

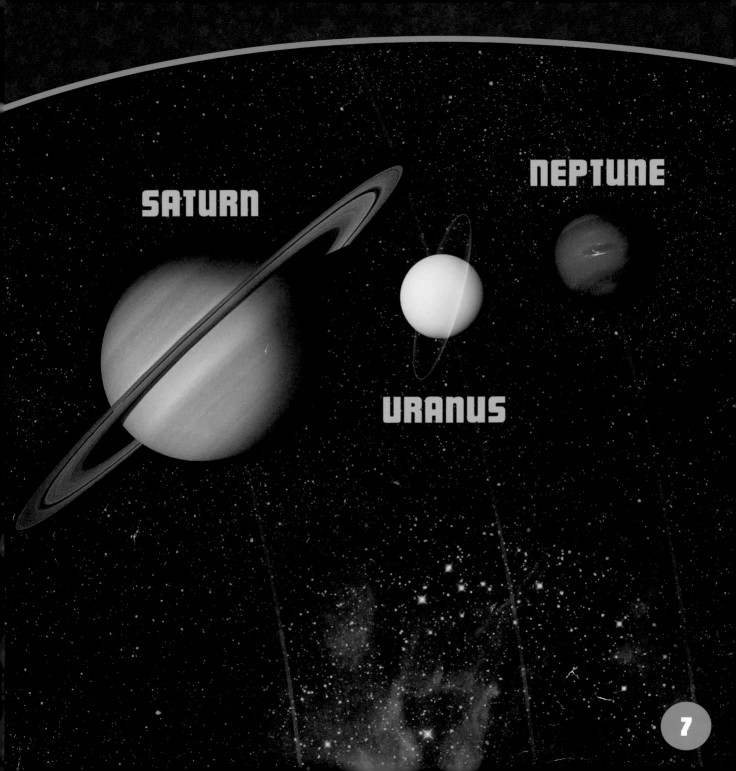

SATURN

URANUS

NEPTUNE

The Moon is much smaller than Earth.

About 50 of our Moons could fit inside Earth.

moon

EARTH

Light from the Sun shines on the Moon.

Light from the Sun

sun

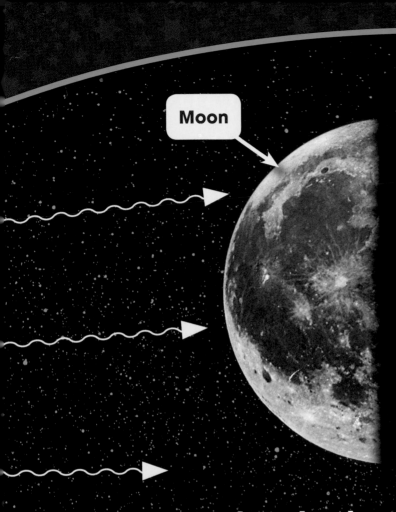

The light makes the Moon look bright in the night sky.

11

The part of the Moon that faces away from the Sun is very cold and dark.

The other side is super hot.

Cold part

Hot part

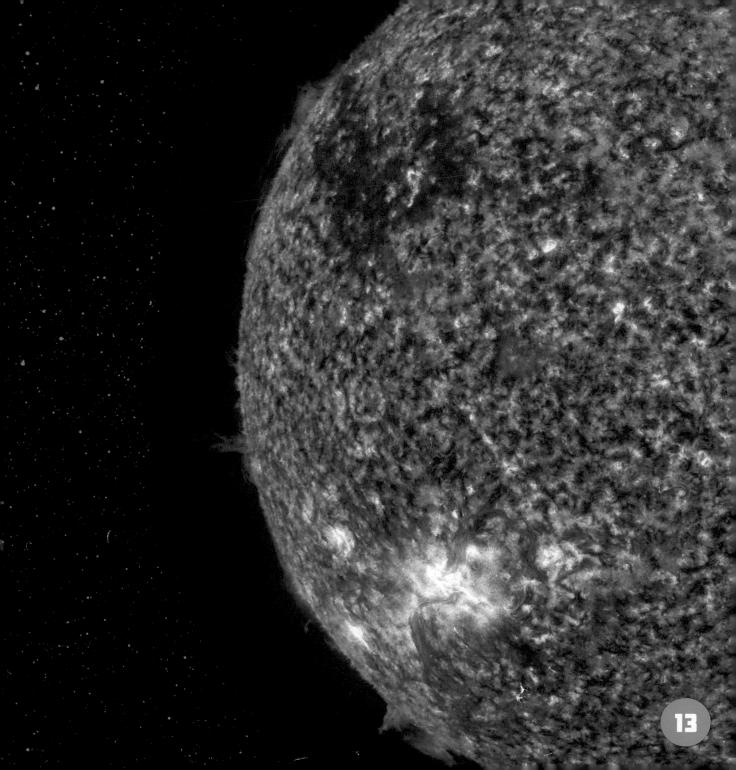

The Moon **orbits**, or moves around, Earth.

Sometimes we see a little sliver of the Moon at night.

Moon

Moon

Other times, we see a big part of it.

The amount depends on where the Moon is in the sky.

Gray rocks and dust cover
the Moon.

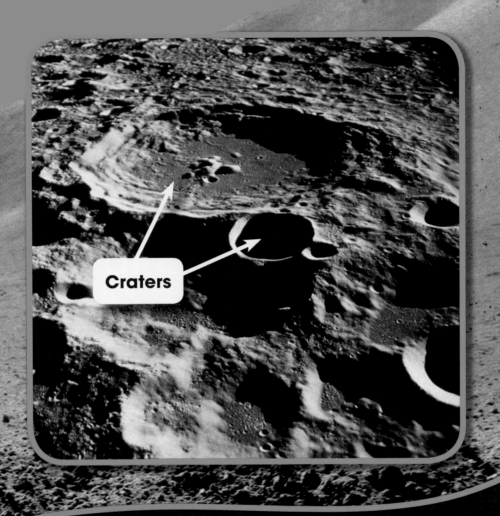

Craters

There are many holes called craters on it.

Astronauts have gone to the Moon in spaceships.

The Moon has no oxygen in its atmosphere.

Spaceship →

Astronaut on the Moon

Astronauts need special suits to breathe there.

In 1969, astronauts put an American flag on the Moon.

They left footprints.

They brought Moon rocks back to Earth!

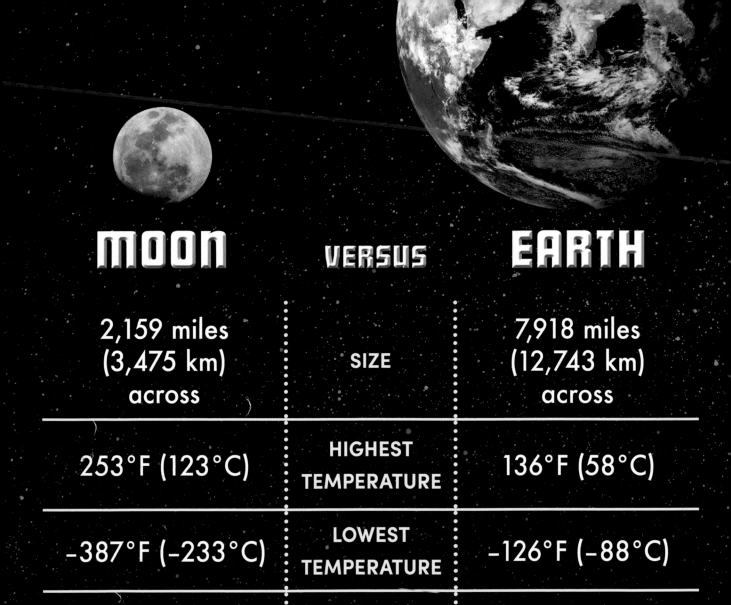

MOON

VERSUS

EARTH

MOON	SIZE	EARTH
2,159 miles (3,475 km) across	SIZE	7,918 miles (12,743 km) across
253°F (123°C)	HIGHEST TEMPERATURE	136°F (58°C)
–387°F (–233°C)	LOWEST TEMPERATURE	–126°F (–88°C)
Dusty and rocky soil, no water	SURFACE	Mostly oceans, some land

GLOSSARY

astronauts (AS-truh-nots) people who travel into space

atmosphere (AT-muhss-fihr) layers of gases that surround a planet or other body in space

craters (KRAY-turz) holes shaped like bowls

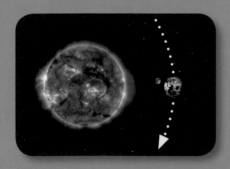

orbits (OR-bits) circles around a planet, the Sun, or another object

oxygen (OK-suh-juhn) a colorless gas found in Earth's water and air, which people and animals need to breathe

Solar System (SOH-lur SISS-tuhm) the Sun and everything that circles around it, including the eight planets and their moons

INDEX

READ MORE

Landau, Elaine. *The Moon (True Book).* New York: Children's Press (2008).

Lawrence, Ellen. *The Moon: Our Neighbor in Space (Zoom Into Space).* New York: Ruby Tuesday Books (2014).

LEARN MORE ONLINE

To learn more about our Moon, visit
www.bearportpublishing.com/OutOfThisWorld

ABOUT THE AUTHOR

J. Clark Sawyer lives in Connecticut. She has edited and written many books about history, science, and nature for children.